RUDOLF STEINER (1861–1925) called his spiritual philosophy 'anthroposophy', meaning 'wisdom of the human being'. As a highly developed seer, he based his work on direct knowledge and perception of spiritual dimensions. He initiated a modern and universal 'science of spirit', accessible to anyone willing to exercise clear and unprejudiced thinking.

From his spiritual investigations Steiner provided suggestions for the renewal of many activities, including education (both general and special), agriculture, medicine, economics, architecture, science, philosophy, religion and the arts. Today there are thousands of schools, clinics, farms and other organizations involved in practical work based on his principles. His many published works feature his research into the spiritual nature of the human being, the evolution of the world and humanity, and methods of personal development. Steiner wrote some 30 books and delivered over 6000 lectures across Europe. In 1924 he founded the General Anthroposophical Society, which today has branches throughout the world.

The glorious, radiant light of worlds
urges me from depths of soul
to deliver my life's godly forces up,
setting them free in universal flight;
to leave myself, and trusting seek myself
only in world light and world warmth.

ST JOHN'S

Festivals

Also available:

(Festivals)
Christmas
Easter
Michaelmas
Whitsun

(Practical Applications)
Agriculture
Architecture
Art
Education
Eurythmy
Medicine
Religion
Science
Social and Political Science

(Esoteric)
Alchemy
Atlantis
Christian Rozenkreutz
The Druids
The Goddess
The Holy Grail

RUDOLF STEINER

ST JOHN'S
An Introductory Reader

Compiled with an introduction,
commentary and notes by
Matthew Barton

Sophia Books

Sophia Books
An imprint of Rudolf Steiner Press
Hillside House, The Square
Forest Row, RH18 5ES

www.rudolfsteinerpress.com

Published by Rudolf Steiner Press 2007

For earlier English publications of individual selections please
see pp. 97–8

The material by Rudolf Steiner was originally published in
German in various volumes of the 'GA' (*Rudolf Steiner
Gesamtausgabe* or Collected Works) by Rudolf Steiner Verlag,
Dornach. This authorized volume is published by permission of
the Rudolf Steiner Nachlassverwaltung, Dornach (for further
information see p. 102)

All translations revised by Matthew Barton

*Matthew Barton would like to thank Margaret Jonas, librarian at Rudolf
Steiner House, for her invaluable help in locating volumes used in
compiling this book*

This selection and translation © Rudolf Steiner Press 2007

A catalogue record for this book is available from the British
Library

ISBN 978 185584 174 1

Cover by Andrew Morgan
Typeset by DP Photosetting, Neath, West Glamorgan
Printed by Cromwell Press Ltd., Trowbridge, Wiltshire

Contents

Introduction

I remember an experience that often happened to me as a child, just before falling asleep. Under closed eyelids, in what Dylan Thomas called the 'close and holy dark', I saw myriad forms resembling vegetation multiplying endlessly in all directions as I floated over it, a burgeoning lush growth of foliage. It occurs to me now that this might relate to an experience of what Steiner calls the 'etheric' or 'life' body, composed of dynamic formative forces which we share with the plant world, and which sustain life and growth.

The vegetative, blossoming, fruiting growth of summer, says Steiner, is the earth's sleeping and dreaming. In sleep, certainly, we go 'out' of ourselves, and at midsummer all of nature seems similarly to entice us to follow its unfolding, languorous dream. If we allow this season to work its magic on us we can feel unlocked into a more fluid, uplifted sphere than mundane realities otherwise allow.

But at the same time too, as Shakespeare so beautifully shows in *A Midsummer Night's Dream*, the veils between different worlds seem to grow more permeable and transparent at this season. The sprites and fairies of his midsummer forest intervene in human affairs and make fun of human foibles. In this summery twilight (= two-light) we see double: both the human and the elemental world at once. In going out of ourselves a little more at this season—like the lover, the lunatic and the poet in Shakespeare's phrase—we can suddenly see more, though confusedly perhaps, shining in towards us foolish mortals from a fluid, dynamic, ethereal realm.

Steiner says in these lecture extracts that in ancient times human beings experienced this season as the only moment of the year when the windows of the heavens opened and they were 'lifted' towards their truest eternal being. Yet the message of St John the Baptist, whose festival falls close to the solstice, on 24 June, is that Christ's advent means we are no longer compelled to dream away from physical reality to find our truest essence in some nebulous 'beyond'. Christ's descent through the great solar window into the depths of earthly matter means we can now discover this essential core of being in the flourishing earthly reality around us, and in the individual human heart.

John's birthday is celebrated on 24 June, six months before that of Jesus, at a time when solar forces in the northern hemisphere have reached their climax and must start to wane towards autumn and winter. John, in his own words, must 'decrease' as the Christ spirit 'increases'. At the time of Christ, merely physical forces had grown too weak to sustain humanity's natural vision of its divine origins and sense of connection with spiritual realities. John's baptism by water was a cleansing process that sought to revive the memory of a pre-lapsarian state, when physical forces were most vital and vibrant, and when the earth was young and fresh — a state we can best imagine perhaps by thinking of early childhood. But recalling this state of innocence was, as John knew, no longer enough to offer a way forward. Steiner says that the deed of Christ, the descent of the Holy Spirit into Jesus at the Jordan baptism, gave a wholly new, renewing impetus, firstly for the whole earth and then, into the far future, for every individual who seeks it, out of his own efforts, in ever-deepening awareness. Gradually conquering our narrow, self-focused preoccupations means that the Christ, the universally human, can increase within us.

But perhaps we still need to ask how midsummer festivals, with their wealth of ancient pagan traditions,[1] relate to the figure of St John. Much less attuned and sensitive to nature than folk once were, what does high summer really mean to us? There is a radical difference between the close-knit rural communities of the past and a much more fragmented post-industrial society. In fact, that isolation of distinct and separate, often jostling egos may be the answer. We may long, as Yeats describes and as many of us seek to do in droves every summer, to leave the 'pavement grey' and search out some isolated 'Isle of Inisfree', with its 'lake water lapping with low sounds by the shore'. Such renewal and reconnection seems essential. Yet more than ever we need to go 'out' of ourselves at all seasons, not so much to dream off into the blue but instead wake up into and within the other, which includes (besides other people) animals, plants, even stones and stars—in other words, our whole human, natural and spiritual environment. Imagination is not just a fanciful capacity but carries us out of our narrow compass into these other realities, and it is clearly lack of imagination that allows modern atrocities, great and small, to occur. Perhaps the question could be posed as follows. Can we find ways to go out of ourselves without losing ourselves, to dream wakefully as it were, to lift ourselves out of isolation into realms and realities beyond us without losing awareness, so that the whole environment, society, the cosmos, is reflected ever more truly in each individual? Steiner believes so, and believes that our human future depends on it.

The passages and extracts collected here are just that—longer or shorter extracts from the larger context of whole lectures. Steiner developed his lectures into an art form in the best sense, and the reader is referred to the original, complete lectures for the 'total experience' and context from which these passages are drawn.

Matthew Barton

MIDSUMMER DREAM:
THE EARTH BREATHES OUT

1. Rising Asleep

Extract from a lecture given in Dornach on
2 May 1920

*Like our own day-night rhythm, says Steiner, the earth
sleeps and wakes in its annual cycle, its time of dream and
sleep corresponding to spring and summer. The
flourishing world of plants is, one can say, the earth
dreaming out towards the wider cosmos.*

Now let us examine what is left lying in bed [when
we fall asleep]. What happens to it? It suddenly
becomes plantlike. Its life is comparable to what
takes place on earth from the moment when plants
sprout in spring until the autumn when they die
back. This plant nature springs up and puts forth
leaves in the human being, as it were, from falling
asleep to awaking. We are then like the earth in
summer; and when the ego and astral body[2] return
and the human being awakes, we become like the
earth in winter. So we can say that the time between
waking and falling asleep is our winter, and that
between falling asleep and waking is our

summer... The earth wakes in winter and sleeps in summer. The summer is the earth's sleeping time, the winter its waking time. Outer perception obviously gives a false analogy, presenting summer as the earth's waking time and winter as its sleep. The reverse is the case, for during sleep we resemble blossoming, sprouting plant life, like the earth in summer ...

If we now consider the cosmos, which as we see manifests waking and sleeping, we will find that we have to regard it as a great organism. We must think of what takes place in its constituent parts as organically integrated into the whole cosmos, just as what takes place in one of our own organs is integrated into our organism.

2. Exhaling into Life

Extract from a lecture given in Vienna,
1 October 1923

Again, Steiner compares the seasons to a process in the human organism, this time to breathing. In winter the earth has 'inhaled' most deeply, in spring it breathes out again. Beings of the elemental world – nature spirits – are intimately connected with this rhythm. Such beings, quite foreign of course to modern ideas of nature, were formerly perceived as inhabiting and enlivening every natural realm and element – water, earth, air and light. Perhaps we can think of them as the soul of the earth, alternately breathed out into the wide expanses of the universe, then returning on the winter inbreath to dwell, like Persephone in Greek myth, underground.

[In winter] outwardly, frost and snow cover the ground, and seeds are received back into earth. The earth now withdraws into herself all that is connected with the earth as germination—here ignoring the world of animals and human beings. In contrast to the burgeoning life of spring and summer, winter shows us dying life. But what does this dying life of winter mean in a spiritual sense? It means that spiritual beings whom we call elemental or nature beings (which constitute the life-giving principle, particularly in plants) withdraw into the earth itself and become intimately connected with it. Such is the earth in winter to imaginative perception;[3] it takes into its body, as it were, its spiritual elemental beings and shelters them there. In winter the earth is therefore at its most spiritual, that is, most fully permeated by its elemental beings...

With the coming of spring the relation of these beings to the earth is transformed into a relation to the cosmic environment. Everything in these beings that during the winter had produced a close relationship with the earth itself now becomes related to the cosmos in spring. The elemental beings seek to escape from the earth; and spring really consists of the earth's sacrificial devotion to the universe in letting its elemental beings flow out into it. In winter these elemental beings need to repose in the bosom of the earth; in spring they need to stream up through the air, through the atmosphere — where they are open to spiritual influences from the planetary bodies, from Mercury, Mars, Jupiter and so on. The planetary bodies do not act upon the earth spirits in winter (this begins in spring). And here we can observe a more spiritual cosmic process and compare it with a corresponding but more material one in the human being: our breathing process. We inhale the outer air, hold it in our own body, then exhale it again. Inbreathing, outbreathing — that is one aspect of human life ...

3. Cosmic Desire

Extract from a lecture given in Stuttgart on
15 October 1923

*The human being is a microcosm of the cosmos — looking
outside ourselves we can find phenomena that we reflect
within our own organism. In this excerpt Steiner speaks
of the element of desire in us, which at midsummer finds
its external image in weather phenomena such as accumulating cloud formations, lightning and thunder. In
desire, of course, we dream out of ourselves to inhabit
another. Steiner also speaks of the counter-force to this
desire element, as we move on from midsummer to
autumn, in the phenomena of shooting stars. These correspond to a subtle, iron-related, awakening process in
the human organism.*[4]

Let us recall a number of things I have already
mentioned here. Let us recall how the year's course,
in its regular sequence through spring, summer,
autumn and winter, has a spiritual content; how
spiritual, supersensible occurrences are revealed in
what happens in the course of the year, just as the

human being's supersensible soul and spirit are revealed in what happens in his physical life between birth and death. Let us reflect how, in what appears outwardly and is physically apparent during the year's course—in winter's snow, spring's sprouting, waxing life, in summer's blossoming and autumn's ripening and fruiting— something spiritual is hidden and sustains it. And so let us turn our gaze firstly to what takes place in the yearly cycle from spring to summer and on towards autumn.

Spiritual beings live in all that the earth reveals, in stone and plant, in all creatures. These are not merely some generalized, wishy-washy spirituality, but distinct spirit beings, nature spirits. During winter these nature spirits enclose themselves in the bosom of the earth, are breathed in as it were by the earth and reside within her. When spring comes the earth breathes out her spiritual content, her soul, and these nature spirits ascend. They aspire upwards with the forces of springing, sprouting life; they are active in the life imbued with radiant, sun-warmed air, streaming upwards within it. And as we approach St John's Day and the time of midsummer, then in the heights above us, if we look up to them, a picture is revealed there, embodied in the forms of clouds, embodied mightily also in lightning and thunder, embodied in all the elements of weather above us, of all that lived in the form of nature spirits during winter in the earth's dark bosom.

During winter we must look down to the earth and feel or behold how, hidden beneath the covering of snow, nature spirits are working to ensure that from winter spring will emerge again, and summer, from the productive earth. But in summer, if we look upon the earth, it seems impoverished by the loss of these nature spirits. They have spread out into the wide breadths of the universe, have united themselves with the forms of clouds and everything that human sight encounters in the heavens above. In all the ways I have mentioned they have streamed up into the heights and have taken with them, in extremely rarefied form, extremely fine dilution, what manifests outwardly as crude and lifeless sulphur. And in fact these nature spirits, as they billow and surge in cloud forms and the like during the height of summer, weave and live pre-eminently in the sulphur that is then present there in an extraordinarily subtle way. If we could speed through these high reaches of our earthly world during the height of summer with a sort of tasting-feeling sense, we should be aware of a sulphurous smell, though in a highly dilute, subtle and intimate form. What develops up there, however, under the influence of the sun's warmth and light, is akin to the process that goes on in the human organism when cravings, wishes and emotions come welling up. Those who have the faculty to behold and feel such things know that the nature spirits in the heights at midsummer live in an element which is as much saturated with desire as the desires bound up with the animal nature of the human being — that animal part of us in which we too bear sulphur in very dilute form. We see as it were our lower aspect, what is animalized in us, arching in natural formations above us at the height of summer, filled with the life of nature spirits. What we thus recognize in its sulphurous quality when it weaves and lives in human nature we call the ahrimanic[5] — the ahrimanic actually lives in it. So we can also say that when, at midsummer, we turn spiritual vision towards the heavens, then the ahrimanic is revealed to us in cosmic sulphurous desires.

And now we see how, against this ahrimanic desire element ... an opposing force is present in the cosmos. The power which brings the human being into subjection through his emotions, dragging him down below the human to the animal level, and is revealed in midsummer high above us, meets a counter-force in those remarkable phenomena which fall to earth from the cosmos in the form of meteoric iron. The shooting stars which come so frequently in August ... reveal this counter-force of nature acting against the desire element which is present there at this time ...

Now the human being is truly a microcosm, a little world. Everything that manifests in the wider world outside, in gigantic and majestic phenomena such as meteors, also manifests within us ... And so in a certain way we bear the sulphurous element within ourselves, emanating from our lower animal nature. This sulphurous, ahrimanic element storms through the human organism, stirs up our desire nature, stirs our emotions. We feel it within us and behold it at midsummer high above our heads. We also see how into this over-arching cosmic mist there shoot the iron arrows of meteorites, cleansing and clarifying it, acting as an opposite pole to the animal-like nature of desire ...

4. Blossoming with the Flowers

Extract from a lecture given in Vienna on
1 October 1923

*Building on the idea of 'breathing out' into the wider
cosmos at midsummer, Steiner now turns to the human
being's relationship with nature, urging us to nurture
subtle perception of and deep union with it. By fully
participating in the changing seasons, he says, we can
develop a more devotional attitude towards everything
around us.*

Advancing from spring towards summer the earth
increasingly loses its inner spirituality. This spirituality, these elemental beings, pass from the earth
out into the cosmos, and fall wholly under the sway
of the cosmic, planetary world. In a former epoch
this was celebrated in the great and profound rites
performed in certain mysteries at the height of the
summer, the season at which we hold the festival of
St John ...

And when summer begins to wane after the St
John season the earth starts to inhale its spirituality

again; and once more the time approaches for the earth to harbour its spiritual nature within itself.

Nowadays we are little inclined to observe this in- and out-breathing of the earth. Human respiration is a more physical process while the earth's breathing is a more spiritual one — the passing out of elemental earth beings into cosmic space, and their re-immersion in the earth. Yet it is a fact that just as we participate inwardly in what goes on in our circulation so we take part in the cycle of the seasons. As the blood circulation inside us is essential for our existence, the circulation of the elemental beings between earth and the heavens is indispensable for us as well; and it is only people's dulled sensitivity that today prevents them from glimpsing how they are affected by this outward cycle of the year ...

Not only the human intellect but the human heart and soul too will gradually undergo a schooling that renders it more sensitive to such impressions. Then people will no longer think that winter is merely the time to put on a warmer coat, or that summer is just the signal for shedding articles of clothing. Instead we will learn to feel the subtle transitions occurring through the year, from the cold snows of winter to the sultry midsummer. We shall learn to sense the course of the year as we do the expressions of a living, soul-endowed being.

Indeed, the proper study of anthroposophy[6] can bring us to the stage when we feel seasonal expressions as the assent or dissent in the soul of a friend. Just as we can perceive in the words of a friend and in his whole attitude of soul the warm heartbeat of a soul-endowed being—whose manner of speaking to us is quite different from that of a lifeless thing—so nature, previously dumb, will begin to speak to us as though from her soul ... we will learn to listen to what the year as the great living being has to tell us, instead of occupying ourselves only with our own narrow compass; and we shall find our place in the whole, soul-endowed cosmos ...

Someone who has gradually acquired this sensitive feeling for nature ... will learn to distinguish between nature consciousness, engendered during spring and summer, and self-awareness which thrives in the autumn and winter. What is nature consciousness? When spring comes the earth develops its sprouting, germinating life. And if I react to this in the right way, if I let all that spring really encompasses speak within me—although I do not have to be aware of it since it speaks in the unconscious depths as well—if I achieve this then I do not merely say that flowers are blooming and plants germinating, but I also feel a true concord with nature, and can say: My higher ego blooms in the flower, germinates in the plant. Nature consciousness is engendered only by learning to participate in all that develops in nature's burgeoning and unfolding life. To be able to germinate with the plant, to bear fruit with the plant, means to pass beyond one's own inner self and become one with nature. The concept of developing spirituality does not mean becoming abstract, but means following the spirit in its developing and unfolding being. And if, by participating in the germinating, the flowering and the bearing of fruit we develop this delicate feeling for nature during the spring and summer, we prepare ourselves to live in devotion to the universe, to the firmament, precisely at the height of summer. Then every tiny glow-worm will be a revelation to us of the cosmos. Every breeze at midsummer will proclaim to us the cosmic principle alive within earthly things ...

FINDING THE GREATER SELF

5. Growing into Cosmic Depths

Extract from a lecture given in Dornach on
31 March 1923

*Ancient initiation enabled people to see in the dynamic
activity of the natural world in summer a reflection of the
human spirit's dynamic origins. Since Golgotha, Christ
has been united with the earth and accompanies the
movement of the seasons — first flowing out into the
cosmos at midsummer, then streaming back from it in
autumn. Thus the seasonal cycle is also, one can say,
contained within the breath of Christ.*

If we carry further our view of the earth's breathing
process during the course of the year, we find the
earth in June ... has completely exhaled. The entire
soul element of the earth has been poured forth into
cosmic space; it is yielded up to cosmic space and is
saturating itself with the forces of the sun, stars and
the planetary bodies. The Christ, who is united with
this soul element of the earth, now unites his force
also with the forces of the stars and the sun, surging
there in the earth soul that is given over to the

universe. It is St John's Day—midsummer. The earth has fully exhaled. In her outer countenance, with which she looks out into the universe, she reveals not her own inherent force, as she did at the time of the winter solstice, but instead reflects from her surface the forces of the stars, of the sun, of all that shines in upon her from the cosmos.

The old initiates, particularly those in the northern regions of Europe, had a very vibrant sense of the inner meaning and spirit of this time of June. At this time they felt their own souls, along with the earth soul, given over to cosmic expanses. They felt themselves to be living not within the realm of earth but rather in the wide breadths of the universe. They said something like this to themselves: 'We live with our soul in the breadths of the universe. We live with the sun and stars. And when we direct our gaze back upon the earth, which has filled herself with springing and sprouting plants, which has brought forth animals of all kinds, then, mirrored and gleaming back to us—from the springing and sprouting plants, the shining, unfolding colours of the flowers, from the insects flitting and creeping hither and thither, the birds of multicoloured plumage criss-crossing the air—we see what we absorb into our souls when we abandon the earth and unite ourselves with the out-flowing breath of the earth in order to live in the far depths of the universe rather than within the earth. What springs and sprouts from the earth in myriad colours is of the same nature. Only it is a reflection, a mirrored energy, whereas in our human souls we bear the original force itself.

If we follow this breathing process still further we come finally to the stage that arises at the end of September. The exhaled forces begin their return movement and the earth inhales again. The soul of the earth, which was poured out into the cosmos, now draws back into the interior of the earth again. Human souls perceive this in-breathing of the earth-soul element—either subconsciously or in clairvoyant perception—as processes within themselves. Those inspired by initiation knowledge of such things were able to say to themselves at the end of September: 'What the cosmos has given us and what has united with our soul force through the Christ impulse we now allow to flow back into the realm of earth, into the earthly sphere which, throughout the summer, served merely as a kind of reflective mirror in relation to the extra-terrestrial cosmos.'

6. Listening for the Answer

Extract from a lecture given in Dornach on
7 April 1923

*Instead of feeling the ego contained within themselves, in
ancient times people felt the core of their being to be
spread out around and above them in the universe. At
midsummer they could come closest to their ego experience through ceremonies involving poetry, music, song
and dance. Such music and dance was like a question to
the cosmos; and the answer for which they listened — like
that wonderfully resonant silence after the first bird sings
at dawn — was experienced as their own true being descending towards them.*

Strange as it may sound to modern people, priests
of the ancient mysteries arranged festivals by
whose unusual effects the human being was lifted
out above the plantlike to the mineral realm,[7] and
thereby at a certain time of year experienced a
lighting up of his ego. It was as if the ego shone
into dream consciousness. You know that even in
a person's dreams today one's own ego is some-

times observed and constitutes an element of the dream.

And so, at the time of the St John's festival, through the ceremonies that were arranged for those who wanted to take part in them, ego consciousness shone in at the height of summer. And at this time people could perceive the mineral realm— at least to the extent necessary to help them attain a kind of ego consciousness, in which the ego appeared as something that entered into their dreams from without. To bring this about, participants in the most ancient midsummer festivals— those of the summer solstice, which have become our St John's festival—engaged in a musical and poetic element, in round dances with a strong rhythmic quality, accompanied by song. Presentations and performances were filled with distinctive musical recitative, accompanied by primitive instruments. Such a festival was wholly imbued with the element of poetry and music. What lived in the human being's dream consciousness was, as it were, poured out into the cosmos in the form of music, song and dance.

Modern people can scarcely have any sense of what was induced through music and song during those intense and widespread folk festivals of ancient times, which took place under the guidance of people initiated into the mysteries. What poetry and music have come to be since then is far removed from the simple, primitive, elemental form of music and poetry that unfolded at the height of summer in those times. Everything that people did then in performing their circle dances, accompanied by singing and primordial poetic recitation, had the single goal of inducing a mood of soul in which occurred what I have just referred to as the shining in of the ego into the human spirit ...

My dear friends, mankind has long ago forgotten why the songbirds sing. It is true that human beings have preserved the art of song and poetry, but in the age of intellectualism, where the intellect dominates everything, they have forgotten the connection of singing with the whole universe ... When at a certain time of year the larks and nightingales sing, what is formed through their singing streams out into the cosmos, not through the air but vibrating in the etheric sphere.[8] It vibrates upwards into the cosmos, up to a certain boundary ... then it vibrates back again to earth, to be received by the animal realm—only now the divine, spiritual essence of the cosmos has united with it.

And thus it is that the nightingales and larks send their voices forth into the universe; and what issues from them comes back to them etherically in the intervals between their singing, now filled with divine, spiritual content. The larks send their voices out into the cosmos, and the divine-spiritual, which is involved in the shaping and forming of the animal kingdom, streams back to the earth on the waves of what had streamed out in the songs of the larks and nightingales.

Therefore if we speak not from the perspective of an intellectualistic age, which sees singing simply as its own reward, but from a truly all-encompassing consciousness, we must say ... that the song that streams forth from a bird's throat into the expanses of the cosmos returns to the earth again as blessing, fertilizing the earth with divine, spiritual impulses which can only work on in the bird world because they reverberate back on the waves of what has been 'sung out' to them into the cosmos.

Now of course not all creatures are nightingales and larks; and of course not all of them sing. But something similar, even though not so beautiful, goes out into the cosmos from the whole animal world. In those ancient times this was understood, and therefore the pupils of the mysteries were instructed in singing and dancing appropriate for this St John's festival — if I may call it by the modern name. Human beings sent this out into the cosmos, of course not now in animal but in humanized form, as a further elaboration of what the animals send out into cosmic space. And something else belonged to these festivals equally: not only the dancing, music and song, but afterwards *listening*. First there was active performance; then people were directed to listen to what resonated back to them. Through their dances and singing, through all that was poetic in their performances, they sent forth a great question to the divine, spiritual cosmos. Their performance streamed up as it were into cosmic space as the earth's water vapour rises, forming clouds above and dropping down again as rain. Thus the effects of the human festival performances arose and came back again—of course not as rain, but as something that manifested itself to human beings as ego strength. People had a sensitive feeling for the transformation which took place in the air and warmth around the earth, at about the time of the St John's festival. Of course nowadays, in our intellectual age, people largely disregard anything like this, having other things to do than people of olden times—going to tea parties and coffee mornings for instance, all sorts of things that are unconnected with the seasons of the year. But in engaging with all these things people overlook the delicate transformation that takes place in the earth's atmospheric environment.

People of olden times sensed how different the air and warmth became around St John's time, at

the height of summer, how these assumed something of the quality of plant life ... They were aware
in their perceptive feeling of a quality of 'greening',
blossoming and fruiting coming towards them not
from the earth but descending from the surround-
ing atmosphere, air and warmth, themselves and
assuming a plantlike character. And when this
happened, these people's consciousness was
transported into the sphere in which the 'I' then
descended, as answer to what they had sent out into
the cosmos in the form of music and poetry.

Thus the festivals had a wonderful, intimate,
human content. A question was sent forth into the
divine, spiritual universe; and people received the
answer because—just as we perceive the earth's
greening, fruiting and blossoming today—they
sensed something plantlike streaming down to
them from the otherwise merely mineral air. In this
way there entered into the dream of existence, into
ancient, dreamy consciousness, also the dream of
the ego.

And when the midsummer festivals were over
and July and August arrived, people had this sense:
'We have an ego, but it remains up there in the
heavens and speaks to us only at St John's time.
Then we become aware that we are connected with
heaven. It has taken our ego into its protection. It
shows it to us when it opens the great window of

heaven at St John's time. But we have to ask about it, sending forth our question into the cosmos in our festival performances ...

You see this whole festival was immersed in musical and poetic elements ... people believed they needed this for life during the rest of the year just as they needed daily food and drink, that they needed to enter into this mood of dancing, music and poetry in order to establish their communication with the divine-spiritual powers of the cosmos ...

And so what people perceived as their being, how they actually sensed themselves, was not acquired simply by being human, but by living together with the course of the year ... Though we have achieved greater freedom in the intellectual age, we are unable to share in this life of the cosmos in the same way that we experienced it in primitive ages. Nevertheless we can approach it, even with our modern consciousness, if we apply ourselves to spiritual realities ... We have acquired our modern consciousness at the cost of losing much of our former connection with the whole cosmos. But once we begin to experience our freedom and world of thinking, we can emerge again beyond ourselves and experience cosmically.

This is what anthroposophy intends when it speaks of a renewal of the festivals.

7. The Ego Shines In

Extract from a lecture given in Dornach on
8 April 1923

*Nowadays our sense of 'ego' has shrunk to a small point
or aperture, like the eye of a needle, through which we
affect the world and allow it to impact on us. Because of
this far greater degree of self-containment within our own
separate skins, it is harder for us than it was for people in
former times to experience worlds of spirit and the moral
forces informing the universe.*

Let us remind ourselves how, in midsummer, the
time we know as St John's, people in ancient times
became aware of a certain relationship to their ego
or 'I' — an ego which they did not yet consider as
exclusively their own, but which they viewed as
still resting in the bosom of divine-spiritual worlds.

Such people believed that by means of the ceremonies I have described they approached their 'I' at
midsummer, while this was hidden from them
throughout the rest of the year ... Only in this one
season, reaching its culmination at St John's, did the

essential nature of their own ego manifest to them, as through a window opening out of the divine worlds of spirit.

Now this essence of the individual ego within the divine worlds of spirit in which it revealed itself was by no means regarded in such a neutral, indifferent — one may even say phlegmatic — way as is the case nowadays. When people speak of the ego today they barely think of it having any special connection either with this world or any other. Rather they consider the 'I' as a kind of point; what someone does rays out from it, and what he perceives rays in. But this kind of ego sense is altogether phlegmatic in nature. We cannot really say that modern human beings feel the 'ego-hood' of the 'I' — despite the fact that it is theirs. If people are honest they cannot really claim to be fond of their ego. They are fond of their instincts and may be fond of this or that kind of experience. But the 'I' itself is just a tiny word which is sensed as a point — in which all I have referred to is more or less condensed. But in those ancient times when, after long preparations, the approach to this 'I' was accomplished ceremonially, each person was able, in a sense, to meet his 'I' in the universe. Following this meeting, then, the 'I' was perceived to be withdrawing again gradually, and leaving the human being alone once more with his physical body and soul ... in those days people felt the 'I' as having a real connection with the entire cosmos, with the whole world.

But what was felt above all else as far as the relationship of this 'I' to the world was concerned did not belong to the natural order, was not something perceived as an external phenomenon. Rather, it was something deemed to be the very centre of the profoundest moral conception of the world. People did not expect great secrets of nature to be revealed to them at this season. To be sure, such secrets were spoken of, but people did not primarily direct their attention to them. Instead they perceived, through feeling, the need to absorb as moral impulse all that is revealed at this time of midsummer, when light and warmth reach their highest point.

This was the season which people perceived as the time of divine and moral enlightenment. And above all, what they wanted to obtain from the heavens as 'answer' to their performances of music, poetry and dance was an earnest revelation from the heavens of moral guidance and impetus.

And when all the ceremonies had been carried out that I described yesterday[9] as belonging to the celebration of these festivals during the season when the sun's heat was hottest and most sultry, if it sometimes happened that a powerful storm erupted, with thunder and lightning, people saw in this the moral admonition of the heavens to earthly humanity.

There are vestiges from this ancient time preserved in images such as that of Zeus, god of thunder, armed with a thunderbolt. Something similar is connected with the German god Donar. That was one aspect. At the same time people perceived nature at this season as being warm, luminous, self-contained and reposing in itself. And they felt that this warming, luminous nature, as it was during the daytime, also remained at night. But they made a distinction here, saying: 'During the day the air is filled with warmth and light. In these elements of warmth and light spiritual messengers live and weave. Through them higher divine beings try to communicate with human beings, try to endow them with moral impulses. But at night, when these higher spiritual beings withdraw, the messengers still remain and reveal themselves in their own way.'

And thus it was especially at midsummer that people perceived the life and sway of nature in the summer nights and summer evenings. And what they felt then seemed to them to be a kind of summer dream whose reality they experienced, a summer dream through which they approached more closely to divine-spiritual beings, one which persuaded them that every natural phenomenon was at the same time the moral utterance of the gods and that all kinds of elemental beings were also active there, revealing themselves to human beings in their own way.

All the fanciful embellishments attending ideas of the midsummer night's dream,[10] of the St John's dream, are what later remained of the wondrous forms perceived in human imagination as weaving on the soul-spiritual plane through this mid-summer period. In every way this was taken to be a divine-spiritual, moral revelation of the cosmos to human beings ...

Through his inner participation in the festivities celebrated at that time the human being knew that he was lifted up above himself into a realm higher than the human, that the deity grasped the hand that the human being reached towards him at this season. Everything that people believed to be divine and spiritual within them they ascribed to the revelations of the time of St John's.

8. Lifting Language Up

Extract from an address given in Dornach on
24 June 1923

All human speech depends not only on physical vocal organs but also on subtler etheric currents. In this sense we can say that our words are, or can be, life-engendering. However, language has adapted so fully to daily human needs and earthly conditions that nowadays it is difficult to free it again from this orientation. The movement art of eurythmy that Steiner devised seeks to liberate speech by transforming its invisible gestures into movement. This is one way to reclaim the supersensible qualities of speech and remind ourselves of our spiritual nature – an aim also embodied in the St John's festival.

If we consider the fact that in speech and song we really produce a species of gesture through moulding and shaping the out-streaming breath, we shall not be very far from understanding that in eurythmy ... there is a kind of gesture in the moving stream of breath so that something of the nature of speech and song may be brought to expression through movements of the limbs or the entire human body.

We have to realize, though, that the nature of speech will never be understood if we only remain in the physical domain, in our physical organization. We need to see that a higher, supersensible organization is contained within the human physical organization. We must see that the forces which in speech and song give shape and form to the air proceed from the human being's supersensible, etheric[11] organism ...

The organs of speech, and what is produced by them are, of course, primarily a means of human intercourse, and serve the needs of daily life. But the faculty for speaking and singing is something which does not proceed directly *from* the physical organism but rather, if I can put it like this, streams *into* it. In so far as we transcend the physical senses—for as supersensible beings we are masters of our physical sense body—we are supersensibly at work in speech and song even though these activities, manifesting in the physical element of air, are primarily bound up with a physical element. This is why it is possible to bring to artistic expression in speech and song something which corresponds to the yearning in the human being to pass out of the physical world of the senses into the world of spirit—something which is indeed expressed in all forms of art ...

Language ... has absorbed into itself much that is adapted to earthly conditions. We can even say that the development of languages involves their ever-increasing adaptation to the earth.

But if, on the other hand, we free the movements of the human limbs from earthly servitude and devote these movements entirely to the expression of our inner being, to what lies above or outside the things of earth, it then becomes much more possible to express the pure element of soul than is the case in language. Language, especially when it is highly developed, is so well adapted to the things of earth that it is by no means easy to draw it back up into a super-earthly element ...

Today, as an experiment, we will try to express in eurythmy the underlying feeling of the festival of St John. We moderns have grown far away from any understanding of the significance of our connection with the course of the year ... As the summer season of St John approached, people [in olden times] hungered for some celebration of these days of festival which would free them from their earthly bondage. They longed for all such forms of ritual and ceremony as would serve to bring to their awareness the fact that the human being is not merely an exile on earth, but is free to pass beyond it, to expand his vision into the untrammelled spaces of the cosmos, into the ether.

It was this ascent into the spheres of the ether which was celebrated at the season of St John ...

Our festivals have become mere conventions in the sense that we are no longer able to enter into their true mood and feeling. And this is why an art like eurythmy, which is striving to develop from entirely new sources, must point the way towards something entirely new, rather than just 'warming up' what is old.

Nature, however, remains constant. The feeling of the festival of St John remains what it always was. And the visible speech of eurythmy which goes out into the cosmos, the wide reaches of the ether, may be a special means of celebrating and establishing the festivals of the seasons ... eurythmy too must endeavour to play its part in raising our modern humanity out of materialism into a more spiritual atmosphere. And the festival of St John may really help towards this end, for the feeling underlying this festival has always led to the goal of freeing the human being from earthly life through the warmth which pours out from the universe, from the sun to the earth, through the light which is strongest at the height of summer. It is at this season that we can become conscious of standing poised in the cosmos between forces which stream inwards through us from without, and those which stream upwards through us from below.

The mood and feeling of this St John's festival, which has always given the human being an awareness that he is a cosmic as well as an earthly being, may again be employed to raise modern humanity above the merely earthly. And this may best be achieved by means which proceed directly from a spiritual deepening of our modern civilization. One such means is the art of eurythmy.

'HE MUST INCREASE,
I MUST DECREASE'

9. Creating the Vessel

Extract from a lecture given in Munich on
16 May 1912

*The figure of St John stands at the point in the year when
the physical sun has reached its greatest power and
ascendancy and must now wane again as, correspond-
ingly, spiritual light grows in the human being towards
Christmas.*

John the Baptist ... prepares the way for the Christ
impulse. We can see him preparing the way for the
Christ impulse, and we can see how he really
appears to us as the one whose words characterize
this impulse, saying: 'Change your disposition. Do
not look back any longer into the times of ancient
clairvoyance but seek the kingdoms of heaven
instead, in your innermost being!' John the Baptist
characterizes the true essence of the Christ impulse.
He is a herald of Christianity in a truly wonderful
way.

10. From Sense to Spirit

Extract from a lecture given in Dornach on
24 June 1923

*The cycle of the year is a great metaphor for processes at
work in humanity. Science, devoted to sensory reality,
can only carry us to the heights of outward knowledge, as
manifest in technology for instance. St John heralds the
moment of transition between outer and inner explora-
tion, from the sensory to the supersensible.*

We must sense with understanding that the St
John's festival mood is the starting point for that
occurrence which lies in the words: 'He must
increase, I must decrease.'

This means that the impressions upon us of
everything accomplished by empirical research
must decline. As sensory details are increasingly
enhanced, so the impression of the spirit must be
intensified. And the sun of the spirit must shine
more and more into the human heart the more the
impressions of the sense world decline.

The St John's mood must be experienced as the

entrance into spirit impulses and as a departure from sense impulses ... Through the St John's mood we must learn to form our spirit light so that it does not stick like tar to the solid contours of ideas, but finds itself in living, weaving ideas.

11. Cleansing in Water, Renewing in Fire

Extract from a lecture given in Berlin on
10 April 1917

John's baptism of water hearkened back to a lost state of innocence. Yet, as today, looking back offered no ultimate solution. The only way is forward, and this is what John meant by heralding Christ's baptism of 'fire and the Holy Spirit'. Instead of withdrawing into the wilderness, we need to take everything our evolution has given us – the potential for self-development and ego consciousness – and use it to invoke the spirit amidst the often very difficult realities which this same evolution has created. Christ stands before us in this process, as exemplar and guide. He is with us 'until the end of the world'.

Now when John the Baptist was about to baptize Jesus in the Jordan, he said: 'The kingdom of heaven is at hand.' . . . What did John the Baptist do? We are told – and this is clear from the context – that he baptized with water, as he himself said because the kingdom of heaven was nigh. He baptized with water for the remission of sins, saying: 'There cometh one mightier than I ... I have indeed baptized you with water, he shall baptize you with the Holy Ghost.'[12] What is the difference between the baptism by John and the baptism with the Holy Spirit?

... We know that the candidates for baptism suffered total immersion. During this immersion they underwent a kind of loosening of the etheric body, which bestowed on them a temporary clairvoyance ... It was intended that through the loosening of their etheric bodies and the experiences they underwent the candidates for baptism should feel themselves transposed into the condition of consciousness of the time before the 'Fall'. Everything that had occurred since the Fall was to be erased from their consciousness. They were to be restored to their pre-lapsarian state so as to experience the condition of the human being before the Fall ...

Many people at that time felt the urge to return to the age of innocence ... to forego their errant ways, to start life afresh as it had been before the Fall, to refuse to be involved in the changes and developments of the social order and culture, which had taken place up to the time of the Roman Empire or the time of Herod the Tetrarch when John the Baptist was preaching in the wilderness. Those who felt that they must break with the past withdrew from the world and became hermits or anchorites. John the Baptist is a case in point. We are told that his meat was locusts and wild honey, and his raiment was of camel hair.[13] He is depicted as the typical desert father, the typical anchorite ...

At this point we must recall what was said previously about the soul—that since the Fall it had progressively deteriorated, was less and less fitted to perform its function as intermediary between the spirit and the body. This continuous decline could persist for a certain period of evolution, but ultimately had to be arrested. This moment would arrive when spiritual evolution superseded earthly evolution. Men such as John the Baptist had a prophetic intimation of this moment. The time is now at hand, he felt, when souls can no longer be saved, when they must perish without some special dispensation. He realized that either human souls would have to withdraw from life as it had been since the Fall, the cause of their growing decline—in which case earthly evolution would have been in vain—or else something else must intervene. And this realization found expression in the following words: 'He that cometh after me shall baptize you with the Holy Ghost.' John felt that only by withdrawing from the world could people save themselves from the consequences of the Fall. Christ on the other hand wished to save humanity in another way. He wished them to remain in the world and yet still find salvation. He did not want humanity to return to the time before the Fall, but to progress and proceed through further stages of evolution, still participating in the kingdom of heaven.

12. Preparing the New

Extract from a lecture given in Basel on
17 September 1912

John's baptism 'prepared the way' for the coming of Christ. It reminded people of their long-lost spiritual origins, but at the same time heralded a new way forward which called on individuation and a change of heart, a self-transformation of every individual through the power of Christ. Another way to see this, perhaps, is to imagine John as the gateway through which Christ enters: John creates the readiness, the sense of hopeful listening and waiting which is essential for anything new to dawn.

How did this spirit work in John the Baptist? It worked at first, according to the Bible, and especially the Gospel of St Mark, through what is meant by 'baptism'.

What is this baptism really? What was the reason for it? To understand this we have to go somewhat further into what it accomplished. People were submerged under water, and on such occasions a loosening of the etheric body took place.[14] We have often spoken of this as occurring to people exposed to some sudden, life-threatening shock — for instance, if someone falls into the water and is nearly drowned, or if he has a fall while mountaineering. The etheric body partially departs from the physical body, with the result that something happens that always happens to people immediately after death: they see a kind of memory picture of their past life. This is a well-known fact, often described even by modern materialist thinkers. Something similar occurred at the Jordan baptisms. It was not the kind of baptism normal today; at the baptisms by John people were submerged under water, causing the etheric body to be loosened so that they saw more than they could grasp with their ordinary understanding. They saw their life in the spirit, and also the influences affecting it. And they saw the message proclaimed by John the Baptist — that the old times were fulfilled, and that a new age was beginning.

In the clairvoyant perception that was theirs for a few moments during the immersion of baptism they realized that humanity had arrived at a turning point in evolution. What human beings had experienced for long ages under group-soul conditions, had come to an end, and entirely new conditions were needed ... hence the baptism by John led people to realize that they must change their whole outlook ... and look forward to something new: 'The God who can reveal himself within the human ego is drawing near, the divine kingdoms are approaching!'

What was to descend into each separate human heart as the individualized soul was still dwelling in the supersensible world when the time referred to by John drew near ... This spirit which had brooded as it were over mankind and its history would now be able to enter increasingly into each individual heart ... This was contained in the baptism at Jordan when John declared: 'I will make a way for him, will prepare a path for him into human hearts; my spirit no longer merely floats over human beings but will enter their hearts so that *he* may enter too.'

13. The Eternal Awakes in the Temporal

Extract from a lecture given in Kassel on
24 June 1909

The baptism by John, in which the Christ power entered and filled the body of Jesus, is an event very hard for us to grasp. If it is to have any real meaning for us, we have to see it as intimately connected with our own potential for 'rebirth' or the awakening within us of a higher, trans-forming and transformative self. John points to such rebirth through Christ, which is ultimately available to every human soul. The image of a plant – such as St John's wort for instance – may be apt here. Growing leaves through the spring and early summer, it begins to blossom around the solstice. Once it has flowered, as a kind of question to the cosmos, a bee or other insect must descend to fertilize it before a transformation and 'answer' of ripening fruit can occur. Within the inwardness of fruit the seed is formed and ripens towards its new future and potential. Of course this image does not explain the mystery of Christ's deed, since it is drawn from the transient and natural, not the eternal world, and plants have no self-awareness nor any need to develop it.

Nevertheless, nature's metaphors may still offer us a reflection of much vaster spiritual events and processes.

The celebration of a particular festival on the present day of the year was a custom to which a large portion of aspiring humanity once adhered, and it is a matter of importance for the friends of the anthroposophical movement[15] assembled with us in this city that the present series of lectures should begin precisely on Midsummer or St John's Day. As long ago as in ancient Persia a festival known as the 'Baptism of Fire and Water' was associated with a day that would roughly correspond to a day in June at the present time. In ancient Rome the festival of Vesta fell on a similar day in June, and that again was a festival of 'Baptism by Fire'. And if we look back upon European civilization before the spread of Christianity, we again find a June festival which coincided with the time of the year when days begin to shorten and nights to lengthen — when the sun begins to lose a part of the strength it lavishes upon all earthly growth and increase. To our European ancestors this June festival appeared as a gradual withdrawal and disappearance of the god Baldur — who, in their minds, was associated with the sun. In Christian times this same festival gradually became that of St John, the forerunner of

Christ Jesus. Thus it can also be our starting point for the considerations to which we will devote ourselves during the next few days, bearing upon this most important event in the evolution of humanity — upon the deed of Christ Jesus ...

The festival of St John reminds us that the greatest individuality who participated in the evolution of humanity was preceded by a 'forerunner' ... In the course of the development of humanity there occur, ever and again, events of surpassing importance shedding a stronger light than others. We can observe these essential occurrences in epoch after epoch of history, and we repeatedly hear of people who know of them in advance and can foretell their coming. These are no arbitrary events; indeed, whoever has insight into the whole meaning and spirit of human history is aware that such events must come, and knows how he himself must work to prepare for them.

During the next few days we shall often have occasion to speak of the forerunner of Christ. Today we shall consider him from the standpoint that he was one of those who, by virtue of special spiritual gifts, have a deeper insight into things and know that there are pre-eminent moments in the evolution of humanity. Hence he was fitted to pave the way for Christ Jesus. But when we look upon Christ Jesus himself, we clearly realize that the division of chronology into epochs before and after his appearance upon earth is not without good reason. By adhering to this division, humanity to a large extent shows that it has insight into the incisive significance of the Christ mystery. But whatever is real and true must repeatedly be communicated in new forms and new ways, for humanity needs different things from epoch to epoch. Our time needs, in a sense, a new annunciation of this greatest of events in human history, and anthroposophy aims to embody this annunciation ...

You all know the opening words of the Gospel of St John: 'In the beginning was the Word, and the Word was with God, and the Word was a God. The same was in the beginning with God.' The Word or Logos was in the beginning with God, and the Light, it is further said, shone in the darkness but the darkness comprehended it not. This Light was in the world and among human beings, but of those only a small number were capable of comprehending it. Then there appeared the Word made flesh as a man — in a man whose forerunner was the Baptist, John. And now we see how those who had to some extent grasped the significance of this appearance of Christ upon earth are at pains to explain the real nature of Christ. The author of the Gospel of St John definitely indicates that the deepest essence contained in Jesus of Nazareth was none other than the being out of whom all others proceeded, that is, the living spirit, the living Word, the Logos himself.

The other Evangelists were also at pains, each in his own way, to describe what actually appeared in Jesus of Nazareth. The author of the Gospel of St Luke endeavours to show how something far from the ordinary appeared when, through the baptism of Christ Jesus by John the Baptist, the Spirit united itself with the body of Jesus of Nazareth. The same writer goes on to show how this Jesus of Nazareth is a descendant of a line of ancestors reaching far, far back into the past. We are told that the genealogical tree of Jesus of Nazareth reaches back to David, to Abraham, to Adam, and even to God himself . . .

Thus, the individuality who is the bearer of Christ, indeed, the whole advent of Christ, is represented not only as one of the greatest but as the very greatest of phenomena in the evolution of humanity. What is here unmistakably expressed can be put in the following simple words. If Christ Jesus was regarded by those who had an inkling of his greatness as the most momentous figure in the evolution of humanity upon earth, there must be some connection between this same Christ Jesus and the holiest, most essential element in the human being himself. There must be something within us which is in direct correspondence with the Christ event. If Christ Jesus, as is stated in the Gospels, really represents the greatest event in the evolution of mankind, must there not be in all things and in each human soul some bond of union with Christ Jesus? Indeed, the most important and essential point, in the eyes of the Christians of St John and the Rosicrucians,[16] was precisely the fact that in each human soul something exists which directly bears upon and is connected with the events which occurred in Palestine through Christ Jesus. Moreover, if the Christ event may be called the supreme event for humanity, the element that corresponds to the Christ event in the human soul must be the supreme aspect of the human being. What can this be?

The Rosicrucian answer to this question was that every human soul is open to an experience that is expressed by the word 'awakening', or 'rebirth' or 'initiation'. We shall see what is meant by these words.

When we behold, in the world around us, the various things that our eyes perceive and our hands touch, we observe how they arise and decay. We see how the flowers blossom and wither, and how the year's whole vegetation comes to life and dies away; and though there are things in the world such as mountains and rocks apparently defying the ages, the proverb 'A stone is worn by constant water drip' points to a premonition in the human soul that the very rocks and mountains, in all their majesty, are subject to the laws of the temporal world. We know that whatever is formed from the elements grows and then decays; and this applies not only to our bodily form but also to our transient and temporal self. Yet those who know how a spiritual world may be attained are aware that though a person's eyes, ears and other senses do not help in this purpose he may nevertheless enter the spiritual world by way of awakening, or rebirth, or initiation. And what is reborn?

Looking within we can come to the conclusion that what we find in our inner self is the being of which we speak as 'I'. The 'I' is distinguished, by virtue of its very name, from all things of the exterior world. To every exterior thing a name may be applied from outside. We can all call the table 'table', and the clock 'clock'. The word 'I', however, can never resound upon our outward ear if we ourselves are meant, for this word ('I') must be uttered from our inner self. To every other being we are 'you'. This fact in itself enables us to distinguish between our own ego being and all else within and around us. But to this we must add something which the spiritual investigators of all ages have repeatedly emphasized from their own experience for the benefit of mankind — that within this 'I' another, a higher ego is born, as the child is born of the mother.

When we observe human development we see first a child, clumsy in respect of his surroundings, and largely just beholding things. Gradually and by degrees he learns to understand; we see how his intelligence awakens, how his will and intellect grow, and how he increases in strength and energy. But there are individuals who advance also in another way; they attain a higher development. They reach the point, so to speak, of finding a second ego which, looking down upon the first or lower ego, can say 'you' to it, even as the ordinary ego says 'you' to the external world and its own body.

Thus a distant ideal of the human soul can become actuality for those who, following the guidance of a spiritual investigator, say to themselves: 'The self I have so far known participates in the outer world and passes away with it. But a second self slumbers in me — one of which people are not aware, though it is equally united with the eternal as the first self is with the transitory and the temporal.' Upon its rebirth, the higher ego can behold a spiritual world even as the lower ego can perceive the sensory world through the physical senses. This so-called awakening, rebirth or initia-tion is the greatest event the human soul can experience, a view held also by those who called themselves followers of the Rose Cross. They knew that this birth of the higher self, which can look down upon the lower self as a person looks out upon the external world, must stand in connection with the event of Christ Jesus. That is to say: even as an individual can experience a new birth in the course of his development, a new birth for the whole of humanity took place through Christ Jesus. Human individual experience of the birth of the higher ego as an inner, spiritual event is something that was enacted for the *whole* of humanity as an external historical fact through Christ Jesus in Palestine ...

Thus a sharp distinction is necessary here. We have a high initiate reborn through physical lineage as Jesus of Nazareth, and beyond this birth something of significance in the spiritual world — something spiritual which will gradually develop the body until it is ripe for the spirit. When this point is reached, the event thus prepared is enacted. The Baptist approaches Jesus of Nazareth and a higher spirit descends upon him and unites with him; Christ enters the body of Jesus of Nazareth. John the Baptist, as the forerunner of Jesus of Nazareth, might well say: 'I came into the world and prepared the way for one mightier than I. I have preached that the kingdom of heaven is at hand and that human beings must change their heart. I came among human beings and declared to them that a new impulse will enter mankind. As in spring the sun mounts higher in the heavens to proclaim the renewal of life, so I come to proclaim the new life which is the reborn self of humanity.'

When the human principle in Jesus of Nazareth had reached its highest development, and his body had become an expression of the spirit within him, he was ripe to receive the Christ in the Baptism by John. His body had unfolded its full power, as the radiant sun on Midsummer or St John's Day. This had been prophesied. The spirit was to be born out of the darkness, as the sun which increases in power and waxes strong till St John's day and then begins to wane. It was the Baptist's mission to proclaim this and to tell how the sun mounts on high with increasing splendour until the moment when he, the Baptist, could say: 'The Son of the spiritual realms, born of the spirit, behold, he has appeared.' Up to this point John the Baptist was active. But when the days begin to shorten and the darkness again prevails, then, the way having been prepared, the inner spirit light must shine ever more brightly, just as Christ shines forth in Jesus of Nazareth.

Thus did John behold the approach of Jesus of Nazareth as his own increase, as the increase of the sun. 'I must henceforth decrease,' he said, 'as the sun decreases after Midsummer Day. But he, the spiritual sun of Christ, will increase and his light will shine out of the darkness.' Thus did John the Baptist speak of himself and his mission. In this manner the universal ego of all humanity was reborn, fulfilling the condition for the rebirth of the individual higher self in every human being ...

CREATING VISION

14. The Opening Lotus

Extract from 'Advice on Meditation' (undated)
given to pupils of Steiner's esoteric classes

*Though not directly related by Steiner to the midsummer
season or the festival of St John, this passage speaks of
'living right into' enlivened meditative content, of
creating new organs of perception rather like a plant
which can only form new seed by first flowering to its
fullest extent. The seeds of our future can ripen in us
when we open ourselves to an influx of what is not us.
Here Steiner emphasizes the need to develop a sense of
wonder and gratitude to carry us beyond ourselves into
the mysteries of the cosmos. The vessel we lift to the gods
is formed of such feelings.*

Going through our exercises with devotion and
earnestness is the esoteric means for the loosening
of our body. Through the withdrawal of the etheric
body the physical body begins to resemble a plant
from which the sap is, for a time, withdrawn. The
plant dries up and so too, though one does not see it
physically, the physical body partially dries, and

where it has a tendency to illnesses these appear. But when the etheric body has rightly saturated itself with spiritual truths it draws new forces to itself and these work again in a healing way upon the physical body. We are to reach the point where the 'lotus flowers' unfold in the etheric body through the imprint of the astral body.[17]

We should feel the words of meditation to be as much as possible filled with colour, light and sound. We should feel them through and through, live right into them. Spiritual beings live in colours and tones, and by uniting ourselves with definite sense perceptions definite beings flow into us. Through esoteric work we should assimilate a new thinking, feeling and will. We must let a thought that we think pass over into our feeling and fully penetrate it. The fluctuating thought impressions that come at the moment of waking are the cosmic thinking living in us. We can be in them if our dream is not merely experienced as a reflection, as most are, but as if we were actually inhabiting it, moved in our soul, present in our spirit. Concepts gained on the physical plane are of absolutely no help in penetrating spiritual worlds. All that we may retain is the power of forming concepts, sense of truth and logic; and also the faculty to form new concepts, and the sense for new truths that we will come to know.

What is experienced inwardly in meditation and concentration acts on the astral body[18] as the light on the physical eye or sound on the ear, for these were developed through light and sound. The astral body is reorganized through these inner experiences of meditation; the organs of knowledge for the higher worlds are drawn out of it just as were the physical sense organs through sound and light. These organs, however, will only become permanent in the astral body if they are impressed, imprinted in the etheric or life body. Now as long as the etheric body is within the physical body it is very difficult for the experiences of the astral body to impress themselves upon it. In former ages it was impossible for what had evolved in the astral body through meditation and concentration to be imprinted into the etheric body while this remained united with the physical body. When we consider that the sense world actually only exists for us because the organs of the physical body have been sculpted from it, it will not seem particularly astonishing to hear that such higher organs are also developed within our higher members, the etheric and astral bodies. The higher organs assume form in someone who strives for initiation ...

The important thing is to feel that, independent of our conceptual reason, something thinks within us of which we can say: not I but *it* thinks in me.[19]

Although such thoughts mean little to us at first, we can strengthen and further them through a feeling of gratitude to higher powers. If we say after every such moment, however brief, 'I thank you, powers of the higher hierarchies, for letting me perceive this,' then such feelings of gratitude and awe will allow such moments to increase when higher worlds reveal themselves . . .

Gratitude is the vessel that we lift to the gods so that they may fill it with their wondrous gifts. If in all earnestness we foster the sense of thankfulness, then we develop gratitude and loving devotion to the invisible, spiritual life-givers; and it is the most beautiful way to be led from one's personality to the supersensible if this guidance passes through gratitude. Gratitude ultimately brings us to veneration and love of the life-bestowing human spirit. It gives birth to love, and love opens the heart to the spiritual powers pervading life. If, after every meditation, we summon in ourselves the feeling of gratefulness and reverence—a feeling that we can call a mood of prayer—and be aware of the grace in which we participate, we shall realize that we are on the right path for the worlds of spirit to approach us.

15. The Heights, the Depths and the Human Heart

Extract from a lecture given in Dornach on
12 October 1923

*In this excerpt Steiner, one can say, gathers up the whole
content of this volume and condenses it into vivid,
dynamic imaginative pictures, and the powerful, ethereal
figure of the archangel Uriel as midsummer's presiding
spirit. This figure, hovering in the azure heights, looks
down searchingly on human failings. The powerful
excerpt ends with the image of the Trinity, of the Son
living and weaving between Spirit-father and Earth-
mother principles. But Steiner is also at pains to remind
us that such images must be conceived in living, moving,
musical dynamic, not as anything fixed. As if to under-
line this, he brings his lecture to poetic and musical
summation in a trinity of verses that express the con-
tinual interpenetration of these principles.*

Precisely when nature consciousness is strongest, a
strengthening of people's self-awareness must
occur. But in the glow of summer, for the very

reason that nature consciousness is then at its height, it is all the more necessary for the cosmos — if only human beings are willing — to bring the spiritual to meet them.

We can therefore say that in summer human beings are closely enmeshed in nature but, if they have the right feeling and perception for it, objective spirituality comes towards them from nature's weaving life. To find the essence of the human being during St John's time, at midsummer, we must turn to the objective spirituality in the outer world, present everywhere in nature. Only in outward appearance is nature the sprouting, budding — one might also say sleeping — being that calls forth vegetative growth from the powers of sleep, giving form to a kind of sleeping nature life. But in this sleeping nature, if human beings can only perceive it, the spirit that animates and weaves through everything is revealed.

If, at midsummer, we follow nature with deepened spiritual insight and with perceptive eyes, we find our gaze directed to the depths of the earth itself. We find that the minerals down below display their inner crystal-forming process more vividly than at any other time of year. If we look with imaginative perception into the depths of the earth at St John's Tide we really have the impression that down there are the crystalline forms into which the hard earth consolidates, and which gain their full beauty at the height of summer. At midsummer everything down below in the earth shapes itself into lines, angles and surfaces. To gain an overall impression of it we must picture this crystallizing process as an interweaving activity tinged through and through with a deep blue colour...

We can say: 'Looking down we have an impression of linear forms suffused with blue, and everywhere the blue is shot through with lines that sparkle like silver. Everywhere within the silver-sparkling blue the crystallizing process can be discerned. It is as though nature wishes to reveal her formative power in a wonderfully dynamic design, but one that cannot be seen as we normally see things. It is seen in such a way that we can feel dissolved into the moving pattern, feeling every silver-gleaming line below to be within us, part of us. We can feel that as a human form we have grown out of the blue depths of the earth's crust, and that energy inwardly permeates us through the silver-gleaming crystal lines. All this seems part of our own being. And if we then ask why these silver-sparkling crystalline streams are working within us, and what it is that lives and works there, gleaming silver in the blue depths of the earth, we can realize that this is cosmic will. Gazing downwards we have the sense that we rise up out of cosmic will.

And what do we see if we then look up to the heights? There the impression is of outspreading cosmic intelligence. Human intelligence—as I have often said—has not yet reached a very advanced stage. But the heavens at midsummer give us the feeling that cosmic intelligence is active everywhere—the intelligence not of single, separate entities but of many beings co-existing and dwelling within one another. Thus in the heights we have the outspreading intelligence woven through with light, living intelligence shining forth as the polar opposite of will. And while we feel that down below, in that blue darkness, we experience everything only as forces and energies, up above everything is such that perceiving it we are illumined, permeated with a feeling of intelligence.

And now within this radiant activity there appears—I cannot put it otherwise—a form. When we were speaking of autumn I named Michael as the significant figure who rises before our souls, arising out of the weaving life of nature at that season[20] ... And now for St John's time there appears—to describe it in human language, which can only approximate to the reality—an extraordinary earnest countenance, glowing warmly and emerging out of an all-pervading radiant activity of intelligence. We have the impression that this figure forms its warm body of light out of the radiant intelligence. And for this to happen at the height of summer, something I have already described must occur:[21] the earth's elemental beings must soar upwards. As they do so they weave themselves into the shining intelligence up above, and this receives them into itself. And out of that gleaming radiance the figure I have just described takes shape.

This form was divined by instinctive clairvoyance in ancient times, and we can give it the same name by which it was known then. In summer Uriel appears in the midst of shining cosmic intelligence...

Now the deeds of this embodied cosmic understanding, this cosmic intelligence, are woven in light. Through the power of attraction in the concentrated cosmic intelligence of Uriel, the silver earth forces are drawn upwards from below, and in the light of this inwardly shining intelligence, as seen from the earth, they appear as radiant sunlight, densifying into a glory of gold. One has the immediate feeling that the gleaming silver, streaming up from below, is received by the sunlit radiance above. And the earth silver — the phrase is quite accurate — is changed by cosmic alchemy into the living cosmic gold weaving in the heights.

If we follow these processes further, during August, we gain an impression of something that complements the form of Michael already des-

cribed ... Whence does Michael, who leads us over
to autumn, to the time of Michaelmas, derive his
characteristic raiment illumined with golden sun-
shine and then inwardly silvered with sparkling
radiance within the golden folds? Where does
Michael acquire this gold-woven, silver-sparkling
raiment? It comes from what is formed in the
heights through the upward-raying silver and the
gold that flows down to meet it, from the trans-
mutation by the sun's power of the silver sparkling
upwards from the earth. As autumn approaches we
see how the silver raised up from the earth and
given to the cosmos returns as gold, and the power
of this transmuted silver is the source of what
happens in the earth during winter, as I have
described.[22] The sun gold, formed in the heights, in
the dominion of Uriel during high summer, passes
back down to weave and flow through the depths of
the earth, where it animates the elements that in the
midst of winter seek to become the living growth of
the following year ...

We feel a deep longing to understand this
remarkable gaze [of Uriel] directed downwards ...
Its meaning first dawns on the mind when we learn
to penetrate with spiritual vision still more deeply
into the blue, silver-gleaming depths of the earth in
summer. Then we see that here are other shapes
interweaving around the silver-gleaming crystal-

line lines of force. They are, one can almost say, disturbances which continually gather and dissolve.

Then we come to perceive — each person will see this a little differently — that these shapes and disturbances are human errors, contrasting with the natural, harmonious order of regular crystals here below. And it is on this contrast that Uriel directs his earnest gaze. Here during the heights of summer he searchingly scans humanity's imperfections, in contrast with the regularity of the growing crystal forms. From Uriel's earnest gaze we gain the impression of a moral order interwoven with a natural order. Here the moral order does not merely exist in ourselves, separate and distinct, as abstract impulses. We usually regard the realms of nature without seeing any particular morality in the growth of plants or the process of crystallization, but now we see how at midsummer human errors are woven into the regular crystals which are formed through natural processes.

On the other hand, all human virtue and excellence rises up with the silver-gleaming rays and is seen as the clouds that envelop Uriel. This enters into the radiant intelligence, transmuted into cloud-shaped creations ...

And now, once we perceive the connection existing between human morality and the crystalline element below, and between human virtues and the shining beauty above, and if we take these connections into our inner experience, the real St John imagination will appear to us...

Above, illumined as it were by the power of Uriel's eyes, the dove. The silver-sparkling blue below, arising from the depths of the earth and bound up with human weaknesses and error, is gathered into a picture of the Earth-mother. Whether she is called Demeter or Mary, this picture is of the Earth-mother. In directing our gaze downwards we cannot do otherwise than bring together in imagination all those secrets of the depths which together compose the Earth-mother of all existence, while in all that is concentrated in the flowing form above we feel and experience the Spirit-father of everything around us. And now we behold the outcome of the working together of Spirit-father with Earth-mother, bearing within it so beautifully the harmony of the earthly silver and the heavenly gold. Between the Father and Mother we behold the Son. Thus there arises this imagination of the Trinity, which is really the St John imagination, the background to which is formed by Uriel, the creative, admonishing Uriel.

What the Trinity truly represents should not be fixed dogmatically in the soul, for then we might gain an impression that such an idea or image of the

Trinity can be separated from the weaving of cosmic life. This is not so. At midsummer the Trinity reveals itself out of the midst of cosmic life, cosmic activity ...

What is experienced pictorially in this way must also come to life through musical tones embodying the poetic motif that plays through our souls when we feel our way towards great Uriel, active in the light, who calls forth in us a powerful impression of the Trinity. The silver gleam that rays up from below, and is revealed in the form-giving beauty of the light above, must be expressed at St John's tide through appropriate musical instrumentation. Thus, through these musical harmonies, we should find our own inner harmony with the cosmos, for in them the secret of our co-existence with the cosmos at St John's tide would resound. All this would have to find voice in music, so that in looking up to the heights we would be looking at the weaving gold of the cosmos, and would see the glowing form of Uriel emerging from the light-filled gold and directing his gaze and his gesture earthwards, as I have described. All this would have to be in continuous, living movement, not a fixed tableau. That would be one motif, a heavenly motif through which we can feel united, on the one hand, with shining, cosmic intelligence.

On the other hand, in the depths, we feel united

with the tendency to fixed form, to what is immersed in the bluish darkness from which the silvery radiance streams forth. Down there we feel the material foundation of active, spiritual existence. The heights become mysteries, the depths become mysteries, and human beings themselves become a mystery within the mysteries of the cosmos. Right into their bones, into their skeletal system, human beings feel the crystal-forming power. But they also feel how this same power is in cosmic union with the living power of the light in the heavens above. They feel how all the morality at work in humanity lives and has its being both in these mysteries of the heights and in these mysteries of the depths, and in the uniting of them both. They feel they are no longer sundered from the world around them but placed within it, united above with the shining intelligence in which they experience, as in the womb of the cosmos, their own best thoughts. They feel themselves united below, right into their bones, with cosmic, crystallizing forces, and they feel these two poles reunited. They feel their death united with the universe's spiritual life, and they feel how this life of spirit strives to awaken and create the crystal forces and the silver-gleaming rays of life in the very midst of earthly death.

All this, too, would have to resound in musical tones which carry these motifs on their wings and make them part of human experience. For these motifs are there. They do not have to be invented; they can be read from the cosmic activity of Uriel ... We live in the mysteries above to which the Spirit-father points, the mysteries below to which the Earth-mother points, and the mysteries that are joined by the fact that the Christ, through the interworking of the Spirit-father and the Earth-mother, stands directly before the human soul as the sustaining cosmic spirit.

What is woven from all these cosmic secrets I will present to you in the following words, which try to express something of what the human being feels, in the midst of all that goes on at midsummer ... Into the first nine lines are compressed the mysteries of the heights, the mysteries of the depths, and the mysteries of the centre—which are also those of our inner human being. And then [in the last 3 lines] we have the whole gathered up as a cosmic statement of these mysteries of the heights, the depths and the centre, resounding as though with organ and trumpet tones:

Mysteries of the heights

See our weaving:
the shining, stirring
warming pulse of living.

Mysteries of the depths

Let what sustains earth,
and form created in breath
live as true essence holding sway.

Mysteries of the centre and the inner human being

Feel your human bones
shone through with heavenly tones
as joined worlds holding sway.

*Like a cosmic affirmation of these mysteries, sounding
into the whole as though with organ and trumpet tones*

Substance grows dense, is crystallized,
addressed and mended are errors and lies,
hearts are sifted, clarified.

Afterword

In his mysterious and sometimes tortuous *Duino Elegies*, the German poet Rainer Maria Rilke wrestles — the word is accurate — with the human being's physical and spiritual nature, with the whole meaning of 'being here'. The ten elegies, the first words of which, as he relates, were borne to him on the wind, took him many years to complete; and one can feel written into them, like rings in a tree, the effort, pain, joy, insight and despair that he went through as he wrote them.

Elegy Seven[23] seems to me to have particular resonance with midsummer, and with some aspects of St John's which Steiner touches on in this volume. Much of it is concerned with our yearning as human beings, and the colouring of such yearning with not very lofty desires — which cloud our vision and prevent us reaching the ungraspable 'angel'. At the beginning of the elegy, Rilke wrestles with himself to find a way for his cry of 'wooing' to free itself from earthly desires and go soaring into the heights. After the first few lines the poet compares his desires, and desire for response, with the purer season of spring, lifting his song into a beautiful evocation of nature:

No more trying to win hearts, no more wooing;
    let your cry
wean itself and go free. True, you cried pure
like a bird lifted high on the uprush of a season
that almost forgets it hurls a quaking
creature up into the ether, the inscape of the
    heavens,
and not simply a single, whole heart.

                             Your wooing
was that—none other—your wanting
the still invisible beloved to sense you, the silent
girl in whom answer slowly awakens,
warms as she listens; kindles and catches,
fires your feeling with her feeling.
O—and the spring would know this—nothing
does not resonate with promise: starts
with a tentative first questioning call, the pure
day answers *yes* to in far-spreading, rising,
silent stillness. Then song's lifting stages, slow
crescendo to the future's
spires and pinnacles; the warbling, bright,
upwelling fountain that prefigures
fall in its rising, chatter and play, and summer
spreading before it. Not only all the early
    summer mornings,
not only the way they change to day and brighten
with new beginning, not just the days that wrap
a delicacy round flowers; above, embrace

trees' thick girth.
Not just these unfurled powers' devotion,
not just the lanes, not just the evening fields,
not just the breath and clarity after long-
accumulating thunder, not just approaching
    sleep and something
sensed at twilight—but the nights!
Summer's high nights, its stars, earth's crowning
    stars!
O to be dead, and know them endlessly,
    all the stars: for how could we forget them?

Later in the same elegy Rilke, echoing the cry of
St John to 'Change your ways', speaks of the need to
transform and elevate all experience, almost hinting
at the eventual spiritualization of the whole world
from *maya* into invisible reality. Then he speaks of
the confusion that such change in consciousness
brings, how it throws everything out of kilter. His
answer to such confusion is to keep alive a memory
of everything the human race has been through,
built and achieved—all human striving in the face
of time's destructive forces.

Nowhere, my love, will world be but inside us.
Our life goes hand in hand with transformation.
[. . .]
The least change in the world breeds
    dispossessed,

with no hold on the past, nor grasp
of what rushes — though far-off — towards them:
    confounded
they stand there, bereft. But don't be!
Let us just strengthen our hold
on forms we still see. Let us say:
This once stood amongst us, in the midst
of our destiny, of all that destroys, our failure
to see the way we should go; was real and drew
stars down to it from the heavens' sure depths.

But that is still looking back to the past — not to be
forgotten certainly, but not yet a way forward. The
elegy ends with the lone figure of the poet once
more, reminiscent of St John as a 'voice calling in
the solitude' (Steiner says this is more accurate than
the translation 'wilderness'). Here again we find
Rilke struggling, wrestling with his human falli-
bility, yearning for the 'angel' but finding that his
all too human longing acts only to repulse the very
thing he seeks.

Don't think that I'm wooing, angel, and even if
    so —
you won't come. For my call is always so full of
    direction
towards you; against such strong current you
    can't

make any headway. My cry like an arm
    outstretched: my palm
spread out to clutch, stays open before you, as
    though
in repulse and warning,
wide open, ungraspable one.

This feels, to me, like a true picture both of our
current condition and the mission of St John: to
purify our longing so that more and more of the
'angel'—the world of spirit—can enter us. To
decrease so that he can increase. To sing, humanly,
but then fall silent, and listen with every fibre for
the answer which resonates towards us from the
heights and depths of our own being.

Notes

1. Such as leaping over bonfires, collecting water from holy springs or gathering medicinal herbs.
2. In Steiner's view we possess, apart from our mineralized physical body, an etheric or life body which we share with the plant kingdom, and an astral or soul body, related to the stars and cosmos, which we have in common with animals. The etheric body is chiefly associated with rhythms, circulation and habitual ways of doing things, while the astral body is the seat of passions, emotions and soul. The fourth and eternal aspect of our being is the 'I' or ego, which continues to exist after death and subsequently seeks reincarnation in a new body. Apart from the physical body, of course, none of the other bodies are visible to sensory perception. One way to gain a sense of their reality is to try to imagine their absence. Without the etheric or life body, for example, a human being could not live and breathe, since the physical body alone is composed of mineral substance — which is all that is left at death.
3. Quite distinct from 'imaginary', imaginative vision enables us to perceive non-physical realities.
4. See also the companion volume in this series on *Michaelmas*.
5. Lucifer and Ahriman are the two polar forces of evil in Steiner's cosmology. Lucifer tempts us away from

the earth while Ahriman fetters us to it. Christ is the balancing mediator between these two.

6. Anthroposophy was the name Steiner gave to his wide-ranging, Christ-centred philosophy and practice. Literally it means 'wisdom of the human being'.

7. This realm embodies the originating forces from which everything earthly is composed, and is further removed from human consciousness than the plant kingdom. See also: 'The Three Stages of Sleep', lecture given by Steiner on 24 March 1922, published in *Anthroposophy Today*, No. 4, Winter 1987.

8. See note 2 above.

9. See previous extract.

10. This inevitably reminds one of Shakespeare's *A Midsummer Night's Dream* with its fairies and sprites.

11. See note 2 above.

12. Mark 1:5, 7. In Matthew the reference is also to 'fire and the Holy Spirit'.

13. Matthew 3:4.

14. See note 2 above.

15. See note 6 above.

16. The Rosicrucians were an order, founded in the fifteenth century around Christian Rosenkreutz, which pursued a Christ-centred spiritual and meditative path.

17. See note 2 above.

18. See note 2 above.

19. This also relates to the idea of increase/decrease: as the smaller ego falls silent the greater can increasingly resound.

20. See companion volume in this series on *Michaelmas*.
21. See section 3 in this volume.
22. In another lecture in this series.
23. Translation by Matthew Barton.

Sources

Numbers relate to extract numbers in this volume.

1. Dornach, 2 May 1920, in: *Mystery of the Universe*, Rudolf Steiner Press, 2001.
2. Vienna, 1 October 1923, in: *Michaelmas and the Soul-Forces of Man*, Anthroposophic Press, 1982.
3. Stuttgart, 15 October 1923, in: *The Festivals and Their Meaning*, Rudolf Steiner Press, 2002.
4. Vienna, 1 October 1923, in: *Michaelmas and the Soul-Forces of Man*, Anthroposophic Press, 1982.
5. Dornach, 31 March 1923, in: *The Cycle of the Year*, Anthroposophic Press, 1984.
6. Dornach, 7 April 1923, in: *The Cycle of the Year*, Anthroposophic Press, 1984.
7. Dornach, 8 April 1923, in: *The Cycle of the Year*, Anthroposophic Press, 1984.
8. Dornach, 24 June 1923, in: *Eurythmy as Visible Song* (appendix), Anthroposophic Press, 1982.
9. Munich, 16 May 1912, in: NSL 184, typescript in Rudolf Steiner House library archive, London.
10. Dornach, 24 June 1923, in: *St John's Tide*, Mercury Press, 1984.
11. Berlin, 10 April 1917, in: *Building Stones for an Understanding of the Mystery of Golgotha*, Rudolf Steiner Press, 1985.

12. Basel, 17 September 1912, in: *The Gospel of St Mark*, The Rudolf Steiner Publishing Co., 1947.
13. Kassel, 24 June 1909, in: *The Gospel of St John and Its Relation to the Other Gospels*, SteinerBooks, 1982.
14. Place and date not given: extract from 'Advice on Meditation', transcript by Martina von Limburger, in: *Guidance in Esoteric Training*, Rudolf Steiner Press/ Anthroposophic Press, 1994.
15. Dornach, 12 October 1923, in: *The Four Seasons and the Archangels*, Rudolf Steiner Press, 2002.

Further Reading

Rudolf Steiner's fundamental books:

Knowledge of the Higher Worlds
also published as: *How to Know Higher Worlds*

Occult Science
also published as: *An Outline of Esoteric Science*

Theosophy

The Philosophy of Freedom
also published as:
Intuitive Thinking as a Spiritual Path

Some relevant volumes of Rudolf Steiner's lectures:

Christmas
Easter
Michaelmas
Whitsun

The Four Seasons and the Archangels

For all titles contact Rudolf Steiner Press (UK) or
SteinerBooks (USA):
www.rudolfsteinerpress.com www.steinerbooks.org

Note Regarding Rudolf Steiner's Lectures

The lectures and addresses contained in this volume have been translated from the German, which is based on stenographic and other recorded texts that were in most cases never seen or revised by the lecturer. Hence, due to human errors in hearing and transcription, they may contain mistakes and faulty passages. Every effort has been made to ensure that this is not the case. Some of the lectures were given to audiences more familiar with anthroposophy; these are the so-called 'private' or 'members' lectures. Other lectures, like the written works, were intended for the general public. The difference between these, as Rudolf Steiner indicates in his *Auto-biography*, is twofold. On the one hand, the members' lectures take for granted a background in and commit-ment to anthroposophy; in the public lectures this was not the case. At the same time, the members' lectures address the concerns and dilemmas of the members, while the public work speaks directly out of Steiner's own understanding of universal needs. Nevertheless, as Rudolf Steiner stresses: 'Nothing was ever said that was not solely the result of my direct experience of the growing content of anthroposophy. There was never any question of concessions to the prejudices and preferences of the members. Whoever reads these privately printed lectures can take them to represent anthroposophy in the fullest sense. Thus it was possible without hesitation — when the complaints in this direction became too persistent — to depart from the custom of circulating this material "For members only". But it must be borne in mind that faulty passages do occur in these reports not revised by myself.' Earlier in the same chapter, he states: 'Had I been able to correct them [the private lectures], the restriction *for members only* would have been unnecessary from the beginning.'

The original German editions on which this text is based were published by Rudolf Steiner Verlag, Dornach, Switzerland in the collected edition (*Gesamtausgabe*, 'GA') of Rudolf Steiner's work. All publications are edited by the Rudolf Steiner Nachlassverwaltung (estate), which wholly owns both Rudolf Steiner Verlag and the Rudolf Steiner Archive. The organization relies solely on donations to continue its activity.